My First Animal Library

Monkeys

by Cari Meister

Bullfrog Books

Ideas for Parents and Teachers

Bullfrog Books let children practice reading informational texts at the earliest reading levels. Repetition, familiar words, and photo labels support early readers.

Before Reading

- Discuss the cover photo. What does it tell them?
- Look at the picture glossary together. Read and discuss the words.

Read the Book

- "Walk" through the book and look at the photos. Let the child ask questions. Point out the photo labels.
- Read the book to the child, or have him or her read independently.

After Reading

- Prompt the child to think more. Ask: What other things do you think monkeys could do with their hands? Which monkey is your favorite? Why? How do you think monkeys in cold places stay warm?

Bullfrog Books are published by Jump!
5357 Penn Avenue South
Minneapolis, MN 55419
www.jumplibrary.com

Library of Congress Cataloging-in-Publication Data
Meister, Cari.
  Monkeys / by Cari Meister.
    p. cm. — (Bullfrog books. My first animal library, zoo animals)
  Summary: "This easy-to-read nonfiction book tells a story about the many ways monkeys use their hands and how they survive in the wild"— Provided by publisher.
  Audience: 005.
  Audience: K to grade 3.
  Includes bibliographical references and index.
  ISBN 978-1-62031-065-6 (hardcover) — ISBN 978-1-62496-065-9 (ebook)
  1. Monkeys—Juvenile literature. I. Title.
QL737.P9M45 2014
599.8—dc23
                                    2013006899

Series editor: Rebecca Glaser
Series designer: Ellen Huber
Book designer: Heather Dreisbach

Photo Credits: All photos by Shutterstock except the following: Alamy 17, 21, 23tr; Superstock cover, 4, 5, 10, 13, 23ml, 23mr

Printed in the United States at Corporate Graphics in North Mankato, Minnesota.
5-2013 / PO 1003
10 9 8 7 6 5 4 3 2 1

Table of Contents

Handy Hands

Monkeys have hands like people.

How do monkeys
use their hands?

Babies grab their mother's fur.

Time for a ride. Whee!

Monkeys groom each other.

They pick out bugs.

It shows they care.

tool

A monkey holds
a rock.

It is a tool.

He cracks open
a nut. Yum!

Howler monkeys
pull branches.

They make
a tree nest.

Lunch time!

Monkeys use their long fingers to grab fruit and insects.

A spider monkey shakes the trees.

He shouts.

He is warning his troop.

margay

Danger is near.

He saw a hungry margay!

The monkeys swing away.

Their hands grab branches.

The troop is safe now.

Parts of a Monkey

eyes
A monkey's eyes are on the front of its head.

hair
A monkey has hair over most of its body.

hands
Most monkeys have four fingers and a thumb.

tail
Monkeys use their tails for balance.

Picture Glossary

groom
To clean and untangle fur; monkeys groom each other.

spider monkey
A small monkey with long arms and legs like a spider.

howler monkey
A large monkey that has a very loud call.

tool
An item that helps a monkey or person do a task.

margay
A spotted wildcat that lives in forests in Central and South America.

troop
A group of monkeys that live together.

Index

To Learn More

Learning more is as easy as 1, 2, 3.

1) Go to www.factsurfer.com

2) Enter "monkey" into the search box.

3) Click the "Surf" button to see a list of websites.

With factsurfer.com, finding more information is just a click away.